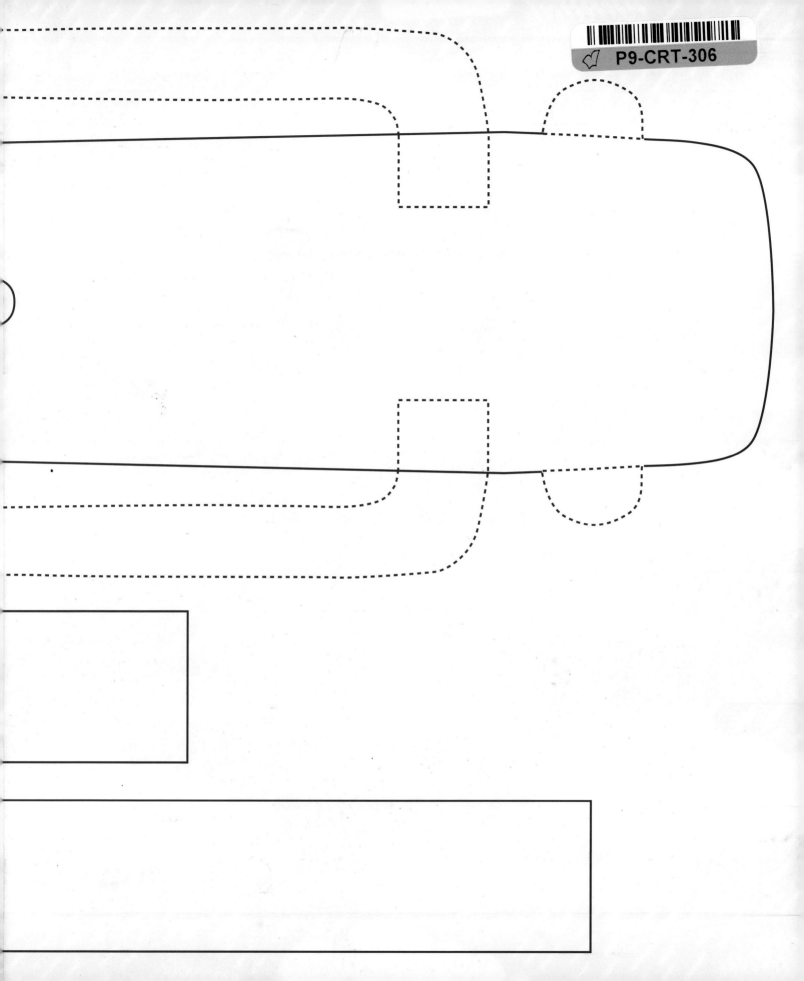

DONNA WILSON'S

CREATIVE CREATURES

KINGFISHER
NEW YORK

SPECIAL THANKS:
I would like to thank my grandma,
Laura Wilson, for encouraging me to be creative
from an early age and for being a great teacher.
I'd also like to thank Kate Beckett, Elaine Gann,
and Erin McIntyre for their creativity and help
with making the props and creatures in
this book, and Gareth for making the
photo shoot such fun.

KINGFISHER
LONDON & NEW YORK

Copyright © Donna Wilson 2013
The activities in this book are copyright protected and must not be created for resale.

Published in the United States by Kingfisher,
175 Fifth Ave., New York, NY 10010
Kingfisher is an imprint of Macmillan Children's Books, London.
All rights reserved.

Distributed in the U.S. and Canada by Macmillan,
175 Fifth Ave., New York, NY 10010

Design: Jo Connor   Editor: Carron Brown
Photography: Gareth Hacker

Library of Congress Cataloging-in-Publication data
has been applied for.

ISBN: 978-0-7534-6947-7

Kingfisher books are available for special promotions and premiums.
For details contact: Special Markets Department, Macmillan,
175 Fifth Ave., New York, NY 10010.

For more information, please visit www.kingfisherbooks.com

Printed in China
1 3 5 7 9 8 6 4 2
1TR/1012/WKT/UG/140MFO

Contents

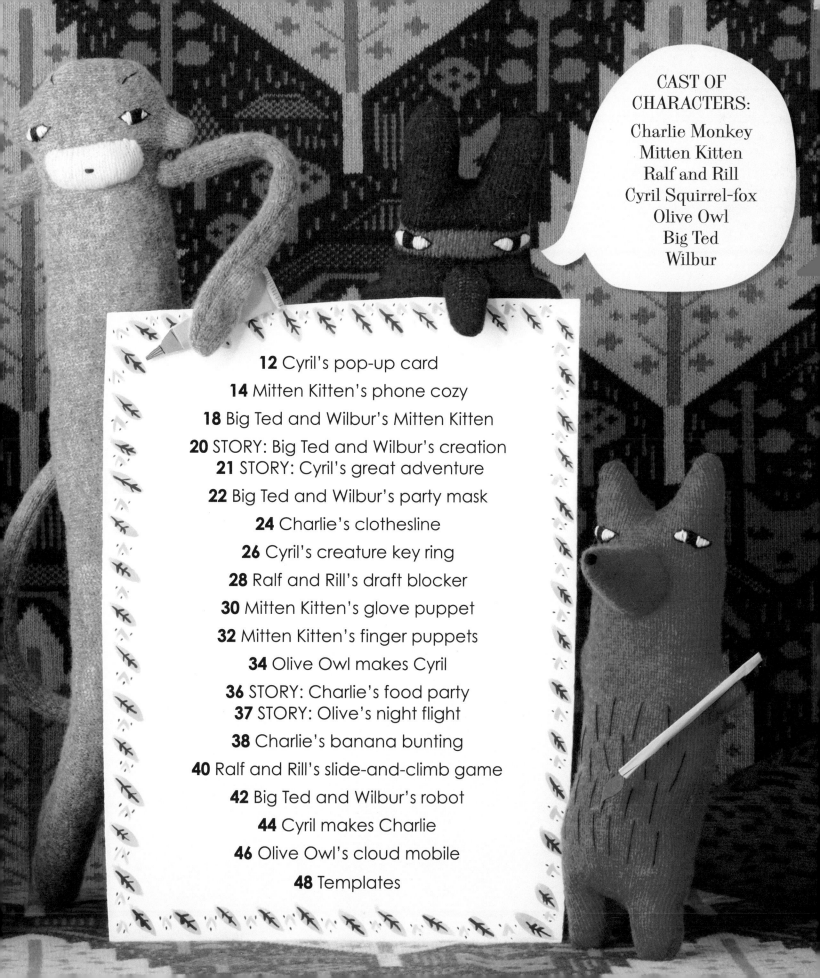

Start creating

Donna Wilson was named Designer of the Year at the British Design Awards in 2010. She set up her own company in 2003 after making knitted creatures at the Royal College of Art in London, England. The handmade creatures and an ever-expanding range of products for the home are now sold all around the world.

If you've ever wondered what your stuffed animals do when you're not in the room, this book will give you an idea. Ralf and Rill create a cleaner-upper robot, Olive Owl designs an owl kite, and Cyril makes a sleeping Charlie Monkey doll. As well as fun friends, there are practical projects, such as a draft blocker, a cell phone cozy, and a handy key ring. Follow the creatures' step-by-step instructions and create until your heart's content.

Sewing tips

You don't have to be a great stitcher to make these projects. To begin sewing, you either tie a knot in the end of the thread or make a holding stitch—a stitch that you stitch over three or four times. I use a piece of thread doubled to make it stronger. Make sure it's not too long or it might get tangled. Always be careful when using a needle.

I used an over stitch on the Charlie doll's arm (see page 45) and all around the wiener dog draft blocker (see page 29). Your over stitching will be seen, but if you make small, close-together stitches, it will look nice and neat.

OVER STITCH

Go over the two edges of the fabric

Needle pushes through from one fabric edge to the other

Needle pushes through the two layers of fabric at the same time

RUNNING STITCH

Runs along the length of the fabric in small stitches

I use a running stitch a lot. It's a quick way to sew two pieces of fabric together. Normally I sew around a shape and turn it inside out so the stitches are hidden. Make the stitches small and close together so gaps can't be seen when the shape is stuffed.

When you see the word "embroider," this means to decorate with stitching.

5

Mitten Kitten's play

Big Ted

Mitten Kitten

Mitten Kitten loves to sing, but her friends just can't stand her high-pitched voice. They always tell her to stop. So, instead of singing, Mitten Kitten decided to direct her very own play. She cast two of her favorite characters, Wilbur and Big Ted, as the lead actors.

Mitten wrote a musical and the pair had to sing, dance, and act—all at the same time! "Let's have a dress rehearsal. Action!" shouted Mitten, who was very excited.

Wilbur was a little nervous at first, but he plucked up all his courage and performed in his loudest, deepest voice. Big Ted had all the moves as he danced around the stage kicking his long legs. They both put on a fantastic performance and didn't even forget any of their lines. Mitten Kitten was so proud—her story had come to life!

Wilbur

Ralf and Rill love playing games and love playing tricks on each other even more. One day, they decided to go for a walk together.

"I'll race you to the hilltop!" shouted Ralf, and he scampered off before Rill could catch his breath. Rill trotted after him, but he couldn't catch up. "I'll race you to the treetop," chirped Ralf, and he leaped from branch to branch. Rill was close on his heels, but he still couldn't keep up. "I'll race you back down!" shouted Ralf. "Wheeeeeeee!" he squealed as he swung to the ground, snapping twigs as he went. Rill flew down the trunk, but still he was too slow.

"I'll race you down the hill!" shouted Ralf. Suddenly, Rill spotted one of Charlie's old banana peels. He jumped on it and with a huge whoosh he slid so fast on the slithery, slippery peel that he overtook Ralf and was first to the bottom of the hill!

Rill

Ralf

Ralf and Rill's slidey race

Ralf and Rill's sock monster

The situation in the sock drawer has gotten out of hand. There are socks everywhere! Ralf and Rill decide to make a sock monster to sort things out.

Your sock monster can have any number of arms and different colored claws.

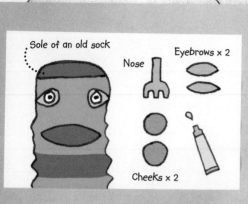

1

Cut out pieces of felt for the cheeks, eyelids, eyebrows, and nose and either glue or sew them into place on the sole part of an old sock. For added monster madness, stick on plastic googly eyes.

Now that you've made one sock monster, try making him some sock creature friends.

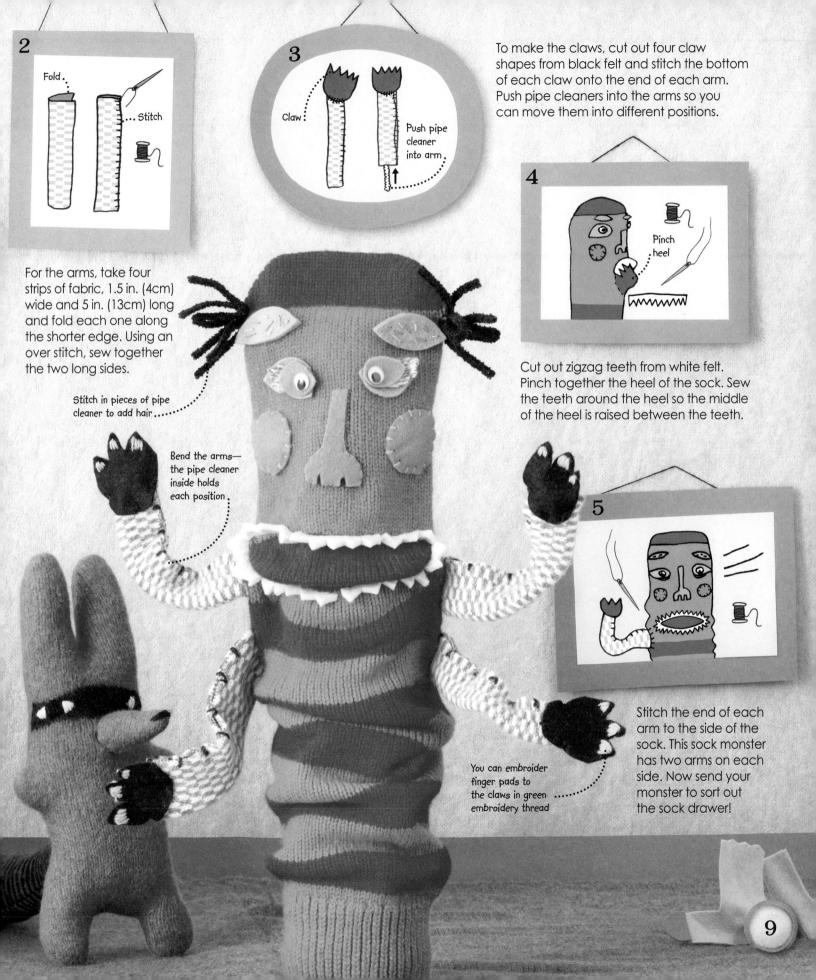

2

Fold

Stitch

3

Claw

Push pipe cleaner into arm

To make the claws, cut out four claw shapes from black felt and stitch the bottom of each claw onto the end of each arm. Push pipe cleaners into the arms so you can move them into different positions.

4

Pinch heel

Cut out zigzag teeth from white felt. Pinch together the heel of the sock. Sew the teeth around the heel so the middle of the heel is raised between the teeth.

For the arms, take four strips of fabric, 1.5 in. (4cm) wide and 5 in. (13cm) long and fold each one along the shorter edge. Using an over stitch, sew together the two long sides.

Stitch in pieces of pipe cleaner to add hair

Bend the arms—the pipe cleaner inside holds each position

5

Stitch the end of each arm to the side of the sock. This sock monster has two arms on each side. Now send your monster to sort out the sock drawer!

You can embroider finger pads to the claws in green embroidery thread

9

Olive Owl's kite

It was a windy day, and Olive needed a friend to fly with. So she decided to make an owl kite out of tissue paper and wire.

How high can you fly your kite?

1

Tape the sharp ends together

Using pliers, bend a thin wire into an owl shape. Carefully tape the sharp ends together to complete the shape. Add a wire crossbar. Secure the center and sides of the bar with tape.

Bend each end of the crossbar back on itself to form a hook around the edge

2

Cut out a layer of tissue paper 0.5 in. (1cm) larger than your kite frame. Snip small cuts about 0.5 in. (1cm) apart all around the frame to form small flaps.

Be careful not to rip the tissue paper

Glue on triangles of different colored tissue paper to give your kite a feathery pattern

5

Knot one end of string tightly around a piece of cardboard. Wind the rest of the string around the cardboard. Tie the other end of the string around the center of the crossbar. Your kite is ready to fly!

Cardboard

4

Cut out shapes from different colored tissue paper to make your owl's eyes, beak, wings, tail, and feathers. Glue these onto the front of the kite.

3

Fold and stick flaps

Fold each small flap over the wire frame and glue it down carefully. Some flaps might overlap, but that is fine.

What you will need

- pliers • thin wire, 24-gauge (0.5mm thick) •
- tape • different colors of tissue paper •
- scissors • clear-drying glue •
- string, 20 ft. (6m) long • cardboard •

11

Cyril's pop-up card

Cyril wanted to surprise Charlie to say thank you for the party Charlie had given him. A pop-up card will do the trick!

1 Fold a sheet of yellow letter-size card stock in the middle and open it out. Decorate the bottom of the sheet with green and blue hills cut out of card stock.

Hill shapes are a good way to create a landscape

Add your message on white speech bubbles.

12

2 Trace the nose template (see page 48) onto orange card stock. Cut out the shape and fold over the two tabs.

Roll into a cone

3 Shape the Cyril nose into a cone. Stick the cone together along the long edge with tape. Color the tip of the nose in marker.

Add a black nose

What you will need
• yellow letter-size card stock • blue, green, orange, and white card stock • scissors • glue • tape • pencil • tracing paper • black pen •

Slits

Fold

4 On orange card stock, draw a Cyril shape that's 9.5 in. (24cm) from ear tip to lower body. Fold Cyril in half lengthwise. Make a slit at either side of the fold above the arms. Insert the nose tabs into the slits and secure the tabs with tape.

Secure tabs on the back with tape

5 Glue Cyril in the middle of the yellow card along the fold, with the two ears sticking out of the top. Stick down the eyes (white card stock with black marker pupils). Fold the card and then open it—the nose will pop out in glorious 3-D!

Draw Cyril's furry chest with a marker

Mitten Kitten's phone cosy

How about...?

To give your phone cozy extra special style, you might want to use two different fabrics—one pattern for the outside and another color for the inner lining.

Mitten Kitten is always on the go, organizing things. Her phone is always with her. She needs a phone cozy to keep it safe.

1

0.5 in. (1cm) gap

0.5 in. (1cm) gap

0.5 in. (1cm) gap

Double the width of your phone

Find two pieces of colored or patterned fabric. Lay one on top of the other and pin at the corners. Lay the phone on top of the layers. Cut the fabric so that it's double the width of the phone and 0.5 in. (1cm) larger at the top, bottom, and left-hand side.

Once inside its cozy, your phone will be less likely to be scratched by claws or other sharp things.

2

Sew together along the bottom edge......

Open out

Sewn edge......

Pin together the two cut-out pieces of fabric. Sew them together along the bottom edge. Open out the fabric so the sewn edge is in the center.

Fold up the opened-out fabric along the longest edge with the seam on the inside. Pin together the corners and sew the fabric together along the longest edge, forming a tube.

3

The seam (the neat join between the two pieces) is on the inside......

Sew together along the longest edge......

4

Lining fabric

Outer fabric......

Turn the tube so that the longest seam is in the center, running top to bottom. The lining fabric is the top half of the tube, and the outer fabric is the bottom half.

What you will need
- fabric, such as from an old sweater •
- ruler • scissors • pins •
- needle and thread • felt • glue •

How about . . . ?

Stitch a ribbon or other long piece of material to each side of the phone cozy so you can hang it around your neck.

Sew along the bottom edge of the tube. Turn the sealed tube inside out so it's the right way around, with the seams on the outside.

6 Tuck the lining into the outer fabric ....

Lining fabric...

Sew together the open edges of the lining fabric and push the lining all the way down to the bottom of the outer fabric pocket to create the body of the cozy.

5

Sew here...

Your phone will fit snugly into its cozy.

7

Cut out triangular ears from felt and sew or glue them to the top of the outer layer. For the eyes, cut two white ovals from felt and sew or glue two black felt pupils in the center of each eye. Sew or stick the eyes below the ears.

With a needle and black thread, embroider lines for the nose and mouth. Stitch on long threads for whiskers. Your phone cozy is now ready to travel!

8

Embroider a nose and mouth using black thread

You could also make a cozy for a book or an MP3 player.

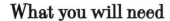
If you can't find polyester toy stuffing, you can use the stuffing from an old cushion or pillow.

Big Ted and Wilbur's Mitten Kitten

Odd socks and odd gloves can be made into new friends! Wilbur and Big Ted found an old glove and made their own Mitten Kitten.

Mitten Kitten's whiskers are stitched-on pieces of yarn

1

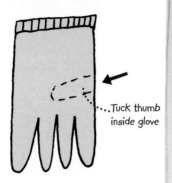

Find an old glove—one that has lost its partner and is not worn anymore. Tuck the thumb inside the body of the glove.

2

After stuffing, sew glove closed

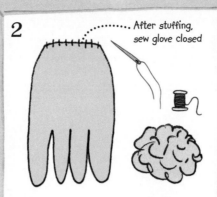

Stuff the glove with polyester toy stuffing, making sure the stuffing goes into all the fingers. Seal in the stuffing by sewing together the open end of the glove.

3

Ears x 2   Nose

Eyes x 2

Collar

Tail

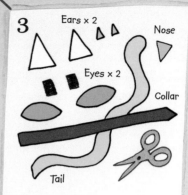

Cut out felt shapes: triangles for the ears, a triangle for the nose, ovals and rectangles for the eyes, and two long pieces for the collar and tail.

4

Using an over stitch, attach the tail to the stuffed glove where the thumb used to be.

5

Embroider the mouth with black thread and stitch on the ears, nose, and eyes. Stitch on some yarn to make whiskers.

6

Wrap the collar around her neck and cut it to fit. Secure the collar by stitching it to the body. Add a small pompom as a bell.

Your Mitten Kitten doll can have a tail of any color or pattern.

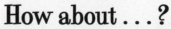

How about . . . ?
Instead of a pompom bell, make a name tag from a piece of yellow or gray felt and embroider a name (perhaps M. K.—Mitten Kitten's initials).

19

Big Ted and Wilbur's creation

Big Ted

Wilbur

Big Ted and Wilbur are both very good at making things, but they never ever like cleaning up the mess they create. "I have an idea," squealed Wilbur excitedly. "Why don't we make a cleaner-upper robot so we never have to clean!" "What a fantastic plan!" agreed Big Ted.

The pair immediately began searching for materials to make the super cleaner-upper robot. Wilbur emptied the kitchen cabinets and found aluminum foil and bottle tops for the robot's buttons. Big Ted trawled through the garage, finding all sorts of cardboard tubes and boxes for the robot's body.

They stuck these materials together, and soon the robot took shape. When Wilbur pressed the "On" button, the robot's eyes opened . . . he took a step forward . . . "Give me your command," said the robot. Big Ted looked around at the mess they had made. "Clean it up, robot!" he commanded. The robot swiveled his head, looked around, and then turned himself off and began to snore. Wilbur and Big Ted had created a robot that didn't like cleaning either!

Cyril's great adventure

Cyril Squirrel-fox's great-grandfather was a famous explorer. He discovered the tallest oak tree in the giant acorn forest. He was also the first to capture a wild wolf using only his quick wit and survival skills.

Cyril felt he could never be as brave or adventurous as his great-grandfather. He preferred to stay indoors! On his way home one day, Cyril realized that he had lost his keys. "Where did I have them last?" he sighed. Puzzled, he retraced his steps.

He walked backward to all the places he'd been that morning. Backward over the wooden bridge, reversing up the maple tree and along its branches, somersaulting down onto Charlie's clothesline with a backward leap to the ground like a gymnast, and backward up the hill to where he started. "That was fun!" he thought. He rummaged in a pile of leaves and spied his keys down a hole! It turns out Cyril is quite adventurous after all. When he got home, he made a fabric Cyril key ring so he wouldn't have to retrace his steps ever again!

You could also try:

- a tree key ring
- a banana key ring
- a leaf key ring

1

Draw a shape on card stock that is slightly larger than your head, with two domes for ears. Add eyes. Cut out the mask, making sure you can see out of the eye holes.

Big Ted and Wilbur's party mask

It's party time again, and Big Ted and Wilbur are having a costume party. All the guests must come wearing a disguise. Here is the mask Big Ted made.

2

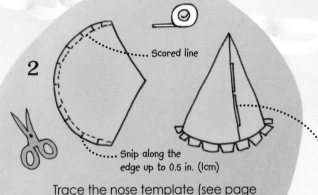

Scored line

Snip along the edge up to 0.5 in. (1cm)

Roll into a cone and tape securely

Trace the nose template (see page 48) onto card stock. Score a line 0.5 in. (1cm) in from the curved edge and snip along the edge. Roll the card stock into a cone and secure with tape.

What you will need

• card stock • pencil • scissors • tracing paper • tape • crepe paper • • glue • elastic •

3

Fold out all the snipped edges to make tabs. Place the nose cone in the center of the mask. Secure the tabs onto the mask with glue or tape.

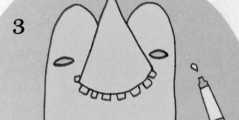

For a simpler version, you can paint or draw on your mask instead of using lots of colored paper.

How about . . . ?
See if you can make different masks for your friends. Maybe some can have card stock hair, triangular ears, or even big, sharp teeth!

4

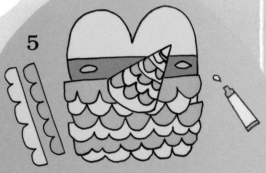

Scalloped edges—cut one edge of each strip into a line of small domes ....

Cut about 20 strips from two colors of crepe paper. Shape one edge of each strip to make scalloped edges.

5

Glue a card-stock strip over the eye holes. Cut eye holes on the strip. On the bottom of the mask, stick a strip of crepe paper. Add more strips above, each overlapping the strip below.

Make sure the pierced holes aren't too close to the edge of the mask ....

6

...Whiskers made from thin strips

Cut thin card stock whiskers and glue them to each side of the nose. Pierce a small hole on each side of the card stock strip on the mask. Thread and knot the elastic so the mask fits securely. You're now in disguise!

Try making a hat for Charlie

Add pieces of paper for patches and fold up the bottom of each leg for cuffs

Cut carefully around Charlie's thin arms and legs

Charlie thinks he might need a bigger tree to live in with all these new clothes!

1

Trace the Charlie template with the arms (see page 48). Copy it onto gray card stock, and cut it out carefully.

2

Cut eyes from white card stock and a mouth area from beige card stock and stick them on Charlie's face. Draw the pupils and a mouth with black marker.

Charlie's clothesline

What to wear today? Charlie always likes choosing his clothes. His favorite outfit is his banana pajamas! Make him paper clothes and see how they fit.

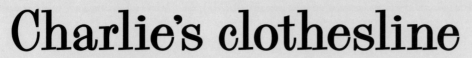

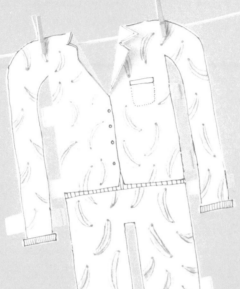

Socks have tabs at the sides and bottom

Create different patterns with markers

How about . . . ?

Here is a selection of Charlie's wardrobe, but what about making him shorts or a T-shirt with a banana picture on the front?

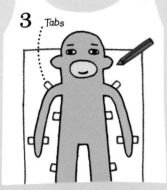

3 Tabs

Draw eyebrows above Charlie's eyes. Lay Charlie on colored paper. For pajamas, draw around his body and add tabs as shown.

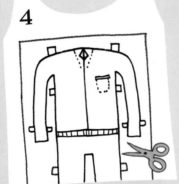

4

Lift Charlie off the paper and connect up the missing parts, such as the neckline. Cut out carefully. Remember not to cut off the tabs!

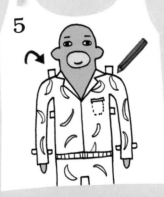

5

Fold over the tabs and hook them over Charlie's body. You can decorate his pajamas with markers. While he's asleep, make him more clothes!

25

Cyril's creature key ring

Cyril Squirrel-fox was always losing his keys. One day he decided to make a large, brightly colored key ring so he would be able to find them anywhere.

With such a bright color of felt, this Cyril key ring is not going to be lost in your bag or pocket.

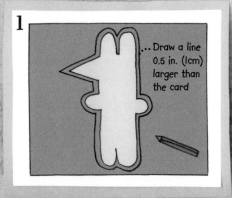

... Draw a line 0.5 in. (1cm) larger than the card

Trace the Cyril key ring template (see page 48) onto thick card stock. Cut it out. Draw around it onto felt, and then draw a line 0.5 in. (1cm) larger all around.

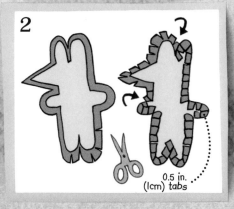

0.5 in. (1cm) tabs

Cut out the felt shape along the larger line. Snip 0.5 in. (1cm) tabs along the edge. Fold over the tabs onto the card stock Cyril and glue them down.

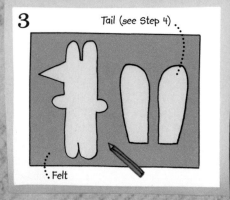

Tail (see Step 4)

Felt

On more orange felt, draw around Cyril again. Cut out this Cyril shape so that it's slightly smaller than the other Cyril shape.

Decorate the tail with stitching

Trace the tail template (see page 48) onto card stock. Cut it out and draw around it twice onto orange felt. Cut out both tails and stitch together.

How about . . . ?
You could stuff the felt shape the way we make the Cyril doll on pages 34–35.

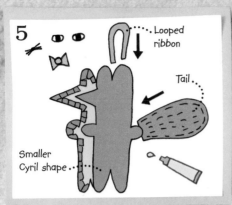

5

Looped ribbon

Tail

Smaller Cyril shape

Using strong glue, attach the tail onto the card stock of the first Cyril shape. Glue a piece of looped ribbon onto the card stock at the top. Stick the smaller Cyril shape onto the back, over the ribbon and the tail. Add thread whiskers, felt eyes, and a felt bow tie. Now you just need some keys!

What you will need

- pencil • tracing paper • thick card stock •
- scissors • orange felt • strong glue •
- pen • needle and thread • ribbon •
- • blue, white, and black felt •

The other creatures are going to be jealous of such a unique key ring!

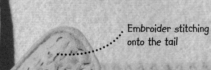

Embroider stitching onto the tail

The felt should be smoothed against the surface of the card stock

Ralf and Rill's draft blocker

In Ralf and Rill's house, the wind gusts through a big gap under the door. A wiener dog will stop those drafts.

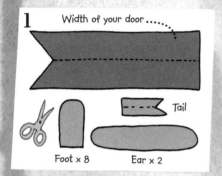

1 Width of your door

Tail

Foot × 8   Ear × 2

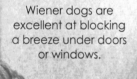

Cut a rectangle of fabric the width of your door for the wiener dog's body. Fold down the middle and cut a diagonal line for a pointy nose. Cut eight identical foot shapes, two tail shapes, and two ear shapes from fabric.

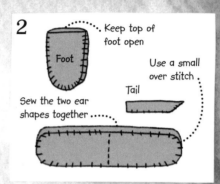

2 Keep top of foot open

Foot

Use a small over stitch

Tail

Sew the two ear shapes together

Sew together the two ears using an over stitch all the way around. Sew the tail in the same way. Sew two of the foot shapes together, leaving the top end open. Repeat for all four feet.

Wiener dogs are excellent at blocking a breeze under doors or windows.

3

Stuff each foot

Stuff each of the four feet. Insert the feet and tail between the folds of the body fabric as shown and pin.

Over stitches should be as close together and as small as you can make them

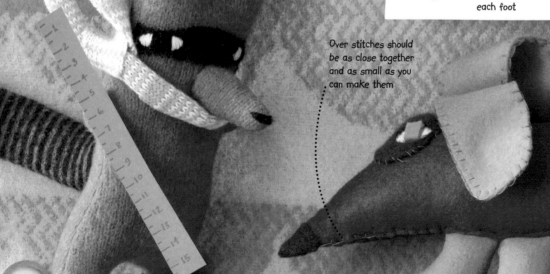

Can you think of any other long animals that would make good draft blockers?

What you will need

- measuring tape • fabric • scissors •
- needle and thread • stuffing (polyester stuffing or old fabric) •
- pins • felt •

Cut a slit on the fold on the top of the head. Fold the ear piece in half and push the center into the slit. Stitch into place.

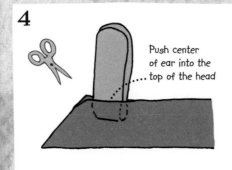

4 Push center of ear into the top of the head

Stitch together all the open sides of the dog's body using an over stitch, leaving a gap in the middle for the stuffing. Stuff the dog as full as you can so he's solid and stiff, and then sew up the gap.

5 Stuffing

6 Add felt features

Add eyes and nose with felt shapes. If you're feeling adventurous, sew on some felt spots! Your dog is ready to stop those drafts!

Mitten Kitten's glove puppet

The musical performance was given by Wilbur the glove puppet. Everyone enjoyed the show!

Paint a backdrop for your theatrical scene or use a patterned blanket.

Try making different glove puppets to create a cast of characters.

Your thumb and little finger will move Wilbur's arms

What you will need
- gray felt • pins • pencil • cotton balls •
- scissors • needle and thread • white felt •
- black pipe cleaner • glue • pink felt •

1

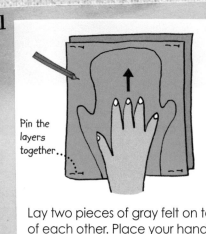

Pin the layers together...

Lay two pieces of gray felt on top of each other. Place your hand on the felt and draw a Wilbur shape around your hand in pencil. Cut out the two layers at the same time.

2

Turn inside out

Stitch together the two layers, leaving the bottom edge open, like a glove. Then turn the stitched felt inside out so the stitching is on the inside.

3

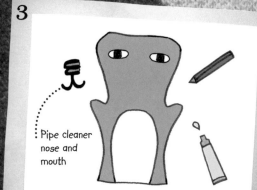

Pipe cleaner nose and mouth

Cut out shapes for the eyes and chest from white felt and stick them on. Draw pupils with pencil. Shape a black pipe cleaner into a nose and mouth and stitch it on.

4

Cotton balls

Stick a white cotton ball to each ear and add a strip of pink felt for the tie. Wilbur is now set for the stage!

Mitten Kitten's finger puppets

The second act introduced two little bears and a cat made out of card stock. Mitten Kitten can fit them on her paws.

What you will need
- card stock • black marker •
- scissors • ruler • double-sided tape •
- ordinary tape •

Features are drawn on with marker.

This puppet has triangular ears and a tail stuck on the back of its body.

How about . . . ?
Make a range of puppets for your fingers: rabbits, robots, and maybe a monster.

1

Cut a rectangle of card stock 1 in. (2.5cm) long and 1.5 in. (4cm) high. Draw a line across 0.5 in. (1cm) down from the top, making two bumps for the puppet's ears. Cut along the line.

2

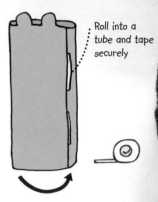

Roll into a tube and tape securely

Roll the card stock around your finger to form a tube that fits snugly. Stick down the overlapping edge with double-sided tape.

3

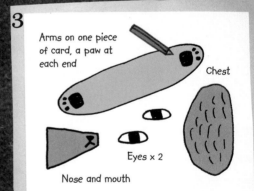

Arms on one piece of card, a paw at each end

Chest

Eyes x 2

Nose and mouth

For the arms, nose, chest, and eyes, cut out shapes from card stock. With a black marker, draw paws on the arms, pupils on the eyes, a nose and mouth, and hair on the chest.

4

Stick arms to the back

Stick the arms onto the back of the finger puppet with tape. Stick on the remaining features with double-sided tape. Let the play begin!

Olive Owl makes Cyril

On a midnight flight through the forest, Olive was surprised to meet Cyril strolling among the trees. He gave Olive the idea to make a Cyril doll once she'd flown home.

1

Pin the fabric together

Reverse of fabric should be on the outside

Front side of fabric faces inside

Layer two fabric pieces. Trace the Cyril template (see page 48) onto card stock. Cut out and draw around the shapes onto the fabric.

2

Gap for stuffing

Gap for stuffing

Stitch around the drawn lines with a running stitch. Leave a 1 in. (2.5cm) gap on both the body and the tail for stuffing.

3

0.5 in. (1cm) gap

Cut out your shapes, leaving a 0.5 in. (1cm) gap between the edge of the cut and the stitched line. Turn your shapes inside out. Poke the ears and feet with a pencil.

What you will need

• fabric • pins • tracing paper • pencil •
• card stock • black and white thread •
• scissors • needle •
• polyester toy stuffing •

4

Sew the gap closed after stuffing

Stuff the tail and body

Use black thread to embroider lines of chest hair

Stuff each shape through the gaps. Sew the gap on the body closed. Embroider the eyes and nose.

5

Bottom of tail

Sew tail onto Cyril's back

Fold in the edge of the tail and stitch it onto the back of your Cyril doll. Your Cyril is ready for a forest stroll (but this time in the daylight)!

Charlie's food party

Cyril

Charlie was hungry! He was planning a surprise party for Cyril and wanted to make it extra special. "What could I use to make the decorations?" he wondered. He looked around him for ideas. "Hmm, we need something bright," he said to himself as he searched . . . All he could see were bananas! Charlie's favorite food is bananas, and he always has a few bunches in his cabinet. "I've got it!" he exclaimed. "Banana bunting! Cyril will love it!"

He got to work with yellow card stock and a ribbon, and soon he had a long line of bananas to hang.

It was spectacular! The first guest was Ralf, who made a few wriggly worms (his favorite food) to add to the bunting. Then Wilbur arrived and made some green leaves. Each new guest added a favorite food, which made Charlie even more hungry!

Eventually Cyril appeared. "Surprise!" everyone shouted. Cyril was so happy with his party and the bunting decorations, and Charlie was very glad that he could start eating.

Charlie

36

Olive

Olive Owl loved the evenings. Just as it was getting dark one day, she flew up through the trees. The wind was in her wings and there were many clouds in the sky. She saw Mitten Kitten in a tree and swooped down. "Hello, Olive! It's going to be stormy tonight!" shouted Mitten. "Maybe you should find some shelter." "I'm not afraid of a drop of rain," Olive replied, and she flew as high as she could. Then there was a rumble of thunder . . . and a HUGE bolt of lightning shot down, narrowly missing Olive. "Whew, that was close!" she thought. "I nearly lost a tail feather!" A little shaken, Olive returned to the tree.

"Are you all right?" asked Mitten Kitten. "Yes! I had no idea storms could be so fierce!" replied Olive. That night, Olive Owl made a mobile to give to Mitten Kitten as a thank you for the warning. She made it shaped like a big rain cloud, but at least this one wasn't dangerous!

You could also try:
- a sun mobile
- a snow mobile
- a lightning mobile

Mitten Kitten

Olive's night flight

Charlie's banana bunting

Feeling hungry? Help Charlie Monkey make his friends a string of paper bananas to hang up in the house.

The card stock monkeys love hanging around the bananas.

1 Fold a piece of yellow card stock in half and draw some banana shapes with black marker.

Use scissors to cut around the banana shapes.

2

Tail needs to be hooked so that it will hang on the ribbon

3 Trace the Charlie body template (see page 48) onto card stock. Draw his arms, ears, and hooked tail separately and then stick them onto the back of the body shape with glue or tape.

Draw on eyes and a smile with
black marker to give your monkey
his very own expression.

4

Hook your bananas over the ribbon, securing
them with glue or tape, and hang the
monkeys between them. Tie each side of
the ribbon to a fence or wall so the bunting
hangs. Now you can party!

5

You could
make other shapes
to hang on your
bunting. What's your
favorite food?

39

Ralf and Rill's slide-and-climb game

Ralf and Rill love playing games.
Sometimes they make up their own.
This one is their version of Chutes
and Ladders.

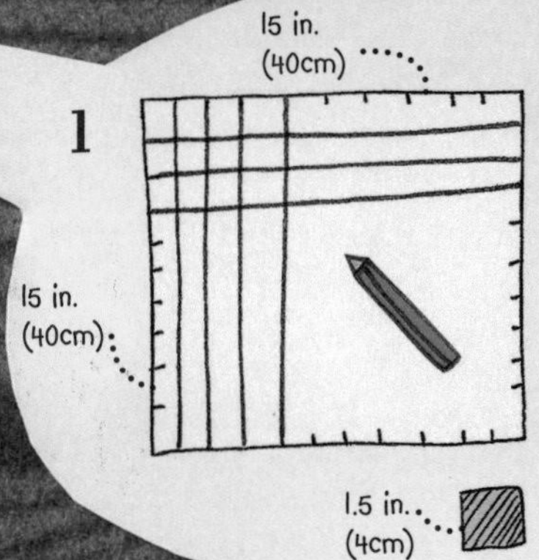

1 Using a ruler, draw a square 15 in. x 15 in. (40cm x 40cm) onto card stock. Mark out intervals of 1.5 in. (4cm) around the edges. Connect the lines lightly in pencil to form a grid. Cut out fifty 1.5 in. (4cm) squares from different colored paper.

15 in. (40cm)

15 in. (40cm)

1.5 in. (4cm)

2 Stick the colored squares onto every second square. Number each square in the grid from 1 to 100, starting at the bottom-right corner.

Make your own creature counters

Place the bananas and trees across the board

40

What you will need
- colored card stock • ruler •
- pencil • scissors • pen • green paper •
- yellow paper • die • glue •

3 Cut out trees from green paper and bananas from yellow paper. Make them all different lengths, from 2 in. (5cm) to 5.5 in. (14cm). In the game, you climb the trees and slide down the bananas.

Add details in pen

4 Stick the trees and bananas so that the top and bottom of each are in the middle of two squares. Space them evenly on the board. Think where they will work best.

Slide down bananas

Climb trees

5 Make some friendly game pieces from colored card stock. Cut out shapes with a rectangular tab at the bottom. Add features to your pieces, fold the tabs, find a die, and start to play!

Fold the tab to make the piece stand

Rules of the game:
Throw the die. Move your game piece the number of squares shown on the die. If a tree trunk is in the square you land on, climb to the square at the tree's top. If you land on a square with the top of a banana, slide down the banana. The first to reach 100 wins.

41

Big Ted and Wilbur's robot

What a mess—empty cartons and scraps of paper everywhere! Big Ted and Wilbur make a robot to help them reuse old boxes and clean up.

1 Tabs · · ·   Fold down tabs · · ·

Snip around the top of two cardboard tubes to make tabs. Fold down the tabs and stick them to the underside of the larger cardboard box to make legs.

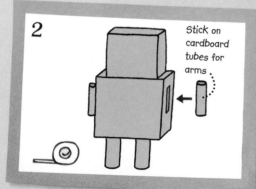

2 Stick on cardboard tubes for arms · · ·

Stick the smaller cardboard box onto the larger box. Stick the side of each cardboard tube arm to either side of the box with double-sided tape or glue.

This robot is one example of what you can do with old packaging. See what else you can create with what you can find around you.

What you will need
- two cardboard boxes • five cardboard tubes (toilet roll tubes) • scissors • cardboard packaging • glue or double-sided tape • foil • markers

Perhaps make card stock tools for your robot.

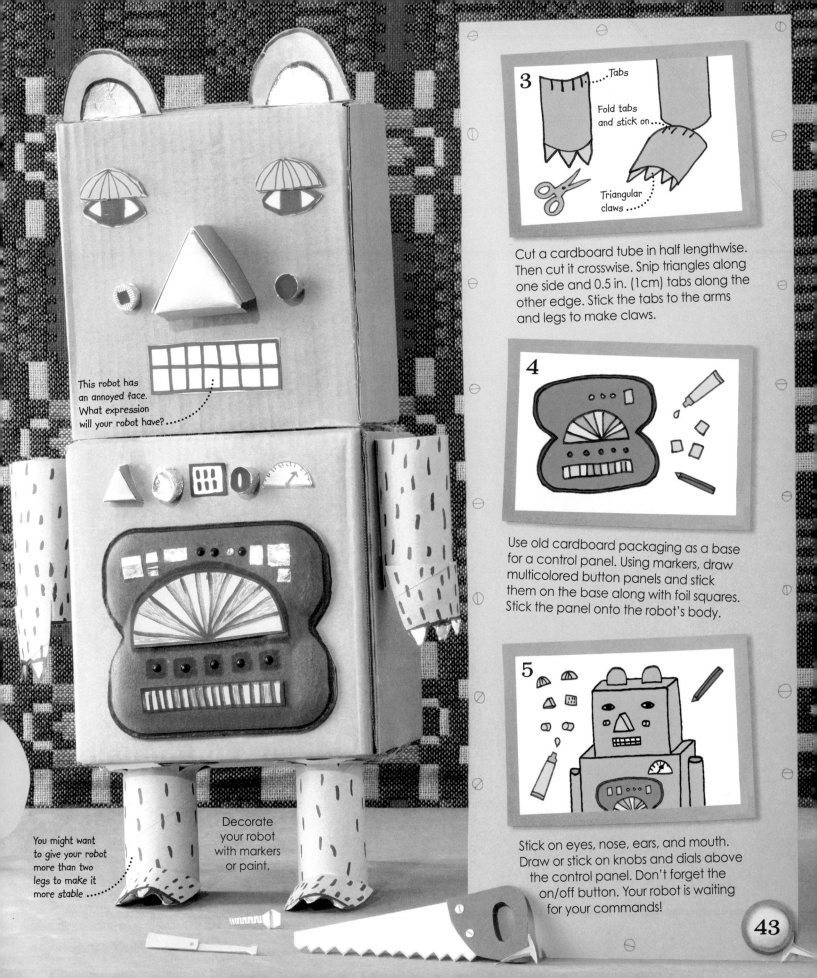

This robot has an annoyed face. What expression will your robot have?

You might want to give your robot more than two legs to make it more stable

Decorate your robot with markers or paint.

3

Tabs

Fold tabs and stick on

Triangular claws

Cut a cardboard tube in half lengthwise. Then cut it crosswise. Snip triangles along one side and 0.5 in. (1cm) tabs along the other edge. Stick the tabs to the arms and legs to make claws.

4

Use old cardboard packaging as a base for a control panel. Using markers, draw multicolored button panels and stick them on the base along with foil squares. Stick the panel onto the robot's body.

5

Stick on eyes, nose, ears, and mouth. Draw or stick on knobs and dials above the control panel. Don't forget the on/off button. Your robot is waiting for your commands!

Cyril makes Charlie

Cyril Squirrel-fox shows you how to make your own sleeping Charlie, but *Ssshhhhh*—you don't want to wake him!

If you want an awake Charlie, add wide-open eyes instead—two ovals of white felt with embroidered black pupils. Or maybe he could be winking?

Make your Charlie doll some bedroom furniture from cardboard.

1

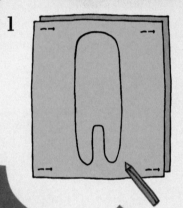

Lay two pieces of felt on top of each other. Pin together. Trace the Charlie body template (see page 48) onto card stock. Cut out the shape and draw around it on the felt.

2

Stitch over the lines on the Charlie doll body and leave a 1 in. (3cm) gap in the side for stuffing. Cut out the shape, leaving a 0.5 in. (1cm) gap between the edge and the stitching. Turn the shape inside out, stuff, and stitch the stuffing gap closed.

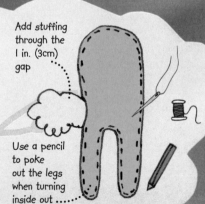

Add stuffing through the 1 in. (3cm) gap

Use a pencil to poke out the legs when turning inside out ......

3

Add a pink paw to the end of each arm.

Roll up each felt rectangle

For the arms and the tail, trace the templates (see page 48) onto gray felt. Cut out and roll. Stitch the long edges closed so they won't unroll. Make paws from pink felt and stitch them onto the arms.

4

Ear

Mouth

Cut out an oval shape from beige felt and two pink ears. Stitch the ears onto the sides of the head and stitch or glue on the oval between the ears. Embroider a mouth and closed eyes.

5

Stitch arms to each side of Charlie's body using an over stitch. Stitch the tail onto the back of the body, just above the legs. Your Charlie doll is ready to take a nap!

Tail

Z Z Z Z Z Z

What you will need
• gray felt • pins • tracing paper •
• pencil • card stock • scissors • needle and
thread • polyester toy stuffing •
• pink felt • beige felt •

Olive Owl's cloud mobile

Olive loves flying around the night skies, especially when it's cool and cloudy. Make a fabric cloud mobile for Olive to fly around in.

Olive Owl's feathers keep her cozy and warm when she's flying.

Your owl can be any color you like. Use a different color for the beak and feet and around the eyes. You could even use old, patterned fabric.

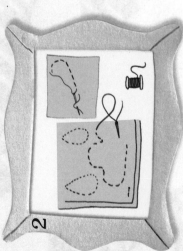

What you will need
- two layers of felt or fabric
- pencil • needle and thread
- scissors • stuffing • ribbon

1

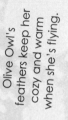

Try pinning the two layers together to stop them from moving

Lay two layers of felt or fabric with front sides against each other. Mark out a cloud, several raindrop shapes and an owl shape with pencil.

2

Using a needle and thread, sew a short running stitch around your marked lines, remembering to leave a gap in each shape to help you turn it inside out.

3

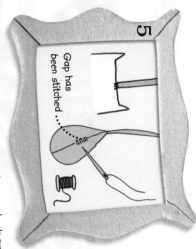

Cut around the outside of each shape, about 0.5 in. (1cm) from the stitching.

4

Push out all the pointed areas with a pencil . . .

Turn your shapes inside out through the gap in each one. Push stuffing into each gap until the shapes are filled, feeling firm and three-dimensional.

5

Gap has been stitched . . .

Neatly stitch up the gaps in each shape to close in the stuffing. Sew pieces of ribbon on the tips of the raindrops and the top of the owl's head.

How about . . . ?

Your owl doesn't have to fly in the rain. Try making a sun mobile with white clouds hanging from it. Or a gray cloud with snow falling from it.

6

Stitch V-shaped marks here to look like feathers

Decorate your owl by cutting out a beak, two feet, and a pair of wings from different colors of fabric or felt. Make your own design to make your owl unique.

7

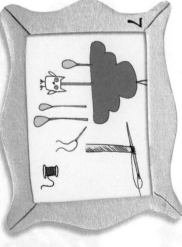

Attach the raindrops and owl to the bottom of the cloud with several layers of stitching. Sew a ribbon to the top of the cloud to hang it with. Let your mobile catch the breeze.

Templates

The templates will help you make some of the creatures. You need to trace them.

How to trace: Lay tracing paper over the template and draw over the line with a soft, dark pencil. Turn over the tracing paper and retrace over the line on the other side. Flip the tracing paper the right way up again and lay it on a piece of card stock or paper. Draw over the line, pressing down hard so that the pencil lines from the back of the card marks the card, leaving a copy of the shape.

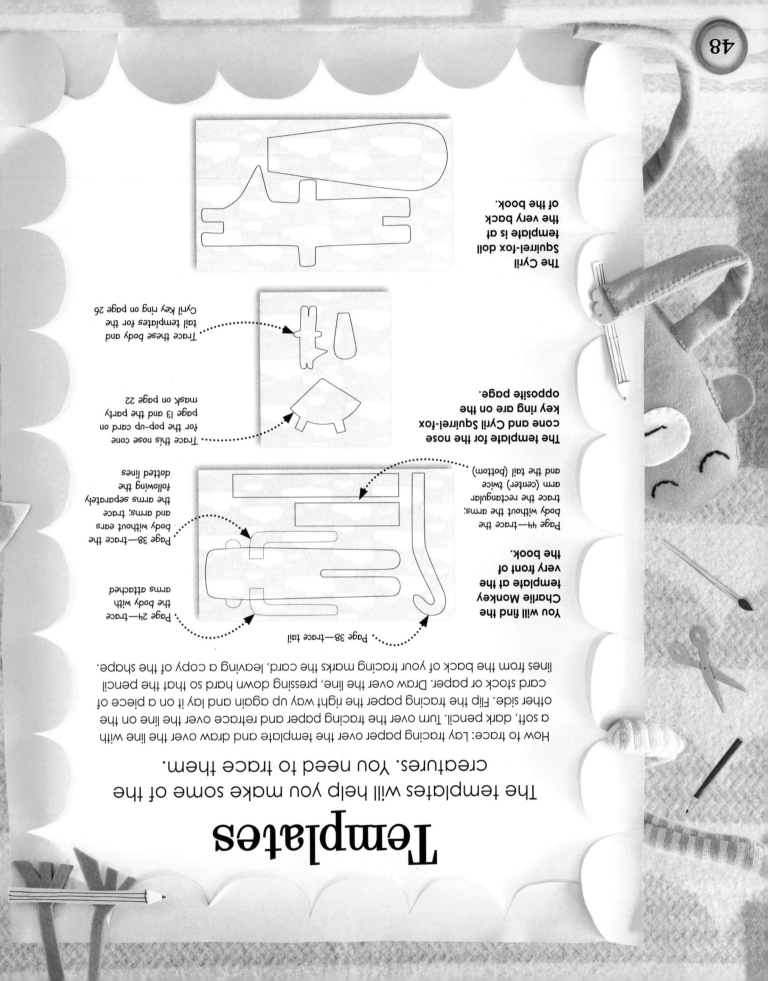

The Cyril squirrel-fox doll template is at the very back of the book.

Trace these body and tail templates for the Cyril key ring on page 26

Trace this nose cone for the pop-up card on page 13 and the party mask on page 22

The template for the nose cone and Cyril squirrel-fox key ring are on the opposite page.

Page 38—trace the body without ears and arms; trace the arms separately following the dotted lines

Page 24—trace the body with arms attached

Page 38—trace tail

Page 44—trace the body without the arms; trace the rectangular arm (center) twice and the tail (bottom)

You will find the Charlie Monkey template at the very front of the book.

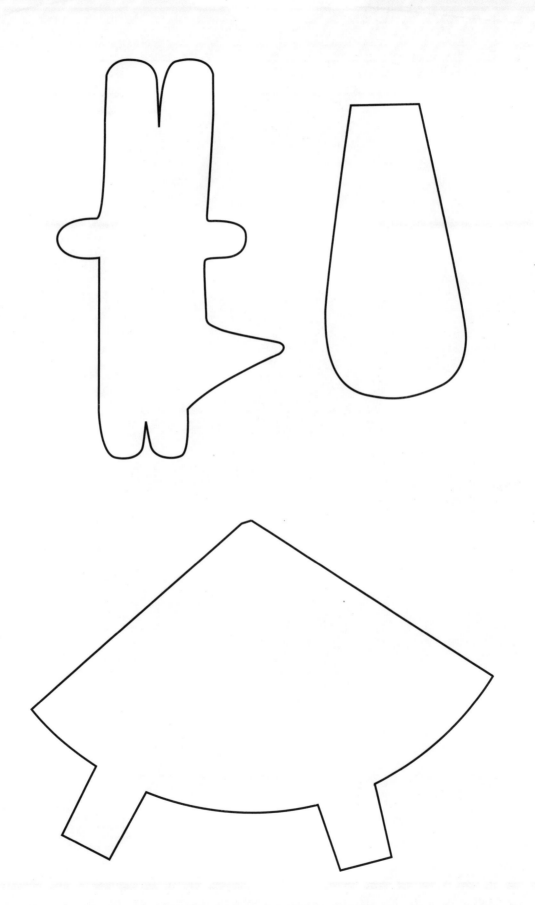